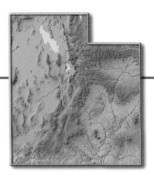

THE BEEHIVE STATE

by Kris Hirschmann

WORLD ALMANAC® LIBRARY

Please visit our web site at: www.worldalmanaclibrary.com
For a free color catalog describing World Almanac® Library's list of high-quality books and multimedia programs, call 1-800-848-2928 (USA) or 1-800-387-3178 (Canada). World Almanac® Library's fax: (414) 332-3567.

Library of Congress Cataloging-in-Publication Data

Hirschmann, Kris, 1967-
    Utah, the Beehive State / by Kris Hirschmann.
        p. cm. — (World Almanac Library of the states)
    Includes bibliographical references and index.
    Summary: Text and illustrations present the history, geography, people, politics and government, economy, customs, and attractions of Utah.
        ISBN 0-8368-5161-7 (lib. bdg.)
        ISBN 0-8368-5332-6 (softcover)
    1. Utah—Juvenile literature. [1. Utah.] I. Title. II. Series.
    F826.3.H57   2003
    979.2—dc21   2002191022

First published in 2003 by
World Almanac® Library
330 West Olive Street, Suite 100
Milwaukee, WI 53212 USA

Copyright © 2003 by World Almanac® Library.

A Creative Media Applications Production
Design: Alan Barnett, Inc.
Copy editor: Laurie Lieb
Fact checker: Joan Vernero
Photo researcher: Dian Lofton
World Almanac® Library project editor: Tim Paulson
World Almanac® Library editors: Mary Dykstra, Gustav Gedatus, Jacqueline Laks Gorman, Lyman Lyons
World Almanac® Library art direction: Tammy Gruenewald
World Almanac® Library graphic designers: Scott M. Krall, Melissa Valuch

Utah

A Desert Paradise

Utah is a rugged place. Most of the state is made up of dry, rocky desert, and the parts that aren't desert are mountainous. Because of this difficult terrain, few early settlers were attracted to the area. Only trappers were willing to brave the harsh land.

The land's very harshness, however, was the eventual cause of Utah's settlement. Utah's first settlers, a religious group called the Mormons, were hoping to build a private paradise in a place no one else wanted. The forbidding Salt Lake Valley fit their requirements perfectly. The Mormons settled in the valley and set to work building an oasis where they could be free from religious persecution.

Perhaps they were too successful. When the Mormons proved that Utah's land could be made fertile, others soon flocked to the area. The discovery of mineral riches in Utah's earth attracted even more people. Transcontinental telegraph wires and railways followed, joining Utah to the rest of the nation and forever destroying the Mormons' treasured isolation.

Today Utah is anything but isolated. A thriving tourism industry brings millions of people to the state each year to enjoy Utah's spectacular national parks and world-class ski resorts. The bustling Salt Lake City airport is an important link between the East and West Coasts of the United States. And thousands of people relocate to Utah each year, making the state one of the nation's fastest-growing regions.

Still, Utah retains much of its heritage. Seventy percent of the state's population is still Mormon. This group dominates Utah's government, schools, and overall culture. In fact, Utah today is the worldwide center of the Mormon faith, which now has more than 11 million members. With such popularity, there is little chance that modern Mormons will be persecuted for practicing their faith. It might be said that they have indeed found the paradise they once sought in Utah's harsh deserts.

▶ Map of Utah showing the interstate highway system, as well as major cities and waterways.

▼ The red mesas and isolated buttes of Monument Valley have formed the backdrop for many western movies.

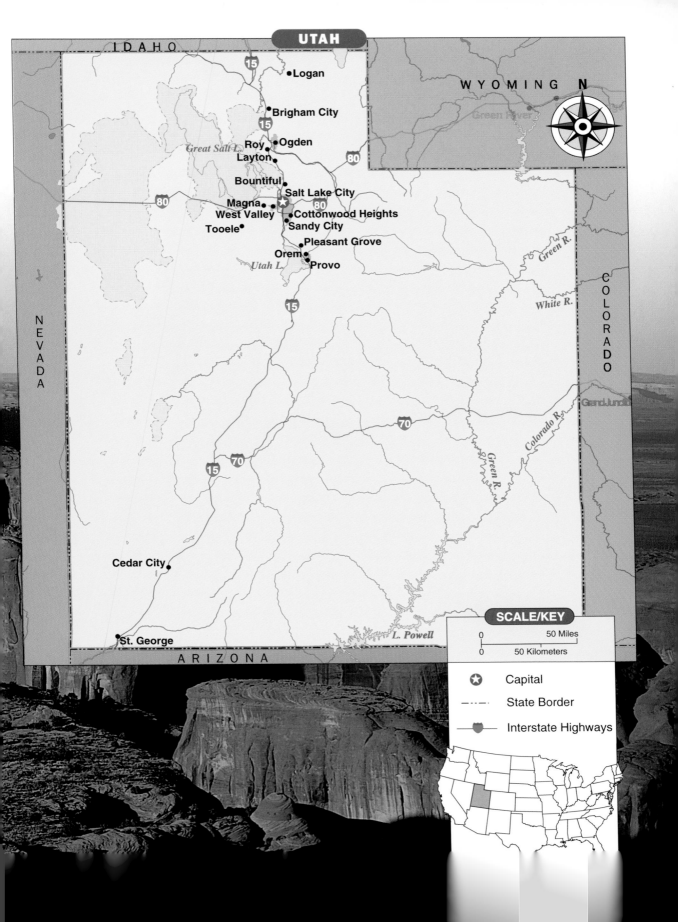

UTAH

IDAHO

WYOMING **N**

Green River

- •Logan

- •Brigham City

- •Ogden

Great Salt L. •Roy

Layton•

Bountiful•

Magna• •Salt Lake City

West Valley• •Cottonwood Heights

Tooele• Sandy City•

•Pleasant Grove

Orem• •Provo

Utah L.

NEVADA

COLORADO

Green R.

White R.

Grand Junction

Colorado R.

Green R.

- •Cedar City

- •St. George

ARIZONA

L. Powell

SCALE/KEY

0 — 50 Miles

0 — 50 Kilometers

⭐ Capital

—··— State Border

🛡 Interstate Highways

Fast Facts

UTAH (UT), The Beehive State

Entered Union

January 4, 1896 (45th state)

Capital	Population
Salt Lake City	181,743

Total Population (2000)

2,233,169 (34th most populous state) — *Between 1990 and 2000, the state's population increased 29.6 percent.*

Largest Cities	Population
Salt Lake City	181,743
West Valley City	108,896
Provo	105,166
Sandy City	88,418
Orem	84,324
Ogden	77,226

Land Area

82,144 square miles (212,753 square kilometers) (12th largest state)

State Motto

"Industry"

State Song

"Utah, We Love Thee" *by Evan Stephens, adopted in 1937.*

State Emblem

Beehive — *To Utahns, the beehive represents the state's founding values of industry and community.*

State Flower

Sego lily — *In the mid-1800s, settlers ate the roots of this flower when crops failed because of a plague of crickets.*

State Tree

Blue spruce

State Grass

Indian rice grass

State Bird

California gull — *In 1848, a flock of gulls devoured a swarm of crickets that were destroying Utah's crops. The gull's status as state bird commemorates this incident.*

State Animal

Rocky Mountain elk

State Fish

Bonneville cutthroat trout

State Insect

Honeybee — *Utah's Mormon settlers called the region "The State of Deseret." Deseret is a Book of Mormon word meaning "honeybee."*

State Fossil

Allosaurus — *Sixty fossilized allosaurus skeletons were found at a single site in Utah.*

State Gem

Topaz

PLACES TO VISIT

Arches National Park, *Eastern Utah*
This spectacular park contains more than two thousand natural rock arches, more than any other place in the world. About half a million people visit Arches National Park each year to hike and enjoy the scenery.

Great Salt Lake, *Northwestern Utah*
With its salty water and sandy beaches, Great Salt Lake resembles an inland ocean. Sailboats, seagulls, and sunny days add to the seaside atmosphere. Public beaches around the lake provide easy access for visitors.

Temple Square, *Salt Lake City*
The majestic Salt Lake Temple and the Mormon Tabernacle are the centerpieces of Temple Square. Drawing more than four million people each year, Temple Square is Utah's biggest tourist attraction.

For other places and events, see p. 44.
For other places and events, see p. 44.

BIGGEST, BEST, AND MOST

- Salt Lake City has the highest per-person consumption of Jell-O in the world.
- Utah's Great Salt Lake is the largest saltwater lake in the Western Hemisphere.
- The Bingham Canyon Mine in Utah's Oquirrh Mountains is the biggest human-made hole on Earth.

STATE FIRSTS

- **1868** Zions Cooperative Mercantile Institution, the nation's first department store, opened in Salt Lake City.
- **1896** Martha Hughes Cannon became the nation's first female state senator when she was elected to the Utah Legislature.
- **1982** A patient at the University of Utah Medical Center became the first recipient of a permanent artificial heart.

Keeping the Past Alive

The Church of Jesus Christ of Latter-day Saints (LDS), which has its worldwide headquarters in Utah, maintains the world's largest genealogical library. The Family History Library is located in Salt Lake City. It was founded in 1894 to help members of the LDS Church (Mormons) research their family histories. Today the Family History Library, which is open to the general public, stores information on more than 700 million individuals. The information is split between databases, microfilm, microfiche, books, magazines, and other formats.

Thrills for All

Lagoon, an amusement park located between Salt Lake City and Ogden, is the nation's second oldest amusement park. The entertainment complex includes a ride section with roller coasters and other thrill rides; a water park with slides, chutes, rapids, and a lazy river ride; a Go-Kart track; a re-created Pioneer Village that takes visitors a hundred years back in time; and more. Summer is the busiest time of the year at Lagoon. During the warm months, an estimated fifteen thousand people come each day to enjoy the park's many attractions.

The Promised Land

> Anything written at the present day which may properly be called a history of Utah must be largely a history of the Mormons, these being the first white people to settle in the country, and at present largely occupying it.
>
> — *Historian Hubert Howe Bancroft,*
> History of Utah, 1540–1886, *1889*

The Utah region's earliest residents were Paleo-Indians, the descendants of people who traveled across a land bridge that once existed between present-day Siberia and Alaska. They roamed present-day Utah thirteen thousand years ago, hunting game and gathering fruits, vegetables, and grains to survive.

Ancestors of Utah's modern Native peoples arrived in the region about fifteen hundred years ago. The two main groups at this time were the Ancestral Puebloans (once called the Anasazi) and the Fremonts. The Ancestral Puebloans are known for building homes in cliffs. The Fremonts lived in pit houses, which were shelters dug into the ground and covered with tree limbs and brush.

Around 1350, the Ancestral Puebloans and the Fremonts disappeared. Scientists are not sure why this happened, but some think a severe drought may have driven the tribes away from their traditional lands. Whatever the reason, other Native groups soon appeared. The Shoshone, Ute, Gosiute, Paiute, and Navajo settled in the Utah region and ruled the land long before the first non-Native settlers arrived.

Native Americans of Utah
Gosiute
Navajo
Paiute
Shoshone
Ute

Early Exploration

The first European expedition to explore present-day Utah set out in July 1776. The expedition was headed by two Spanish friars, Silvestre Vélez de Escalante and Francisco Atanasio Dominguez. The friars hoped to find a convenient trade route between New Mexico and California. Although they failed to find the route they sought, their expedition provided a glimpse of a land previously unseen by Europeans. It also strengthened Spain's claim on the region. Although Spain

DID YOU KNOW?

The Ancestral Puebloans were skilled potters. They left behind many plates, bowls, and other clay objects painted in bold orange, black, and white designs.

made no attempt to colonize or protect the Utah area, the rocky land was considered Spanish territory after Escalante and Dominguez's expedition.

The next influx of white explorers came in the early 1800s. Drawn by the Utah region's large beaver population, American fur traders trickled into the area. The fur traders were known as "mountain men." Some of Utah's most famous mountain men were Jim Bridger, Jedediah Smith, and James Beckwourth. Although the mountain man population was never large — only about a hundred traders were in Utah at any one time — it took a major toll on the local beaver population. By the late 1830s, the mountain men had killed off most of the area's game. They began to leave the state in search of better hunting grounds.

During the mountain-men years, the Utah area passed from Spanish to Mexican possession. Like Spain, however, Mexico made no attempt to govern or colonize the region. The area was still a wilderness — but it was too tempting for the United States to ignore. Although the Utah region belonged to Mexico, the U.S. government began sending army officers into the area in the 1830s to explore.

Joseph Smith and the Mormons

Meanwhile, in New York, the seeds of Utah's future were being planted. Around 1820, a fourteen-year-old boy named Joseph Smith claimed to have had visions from God telling him to restore the true church of Christ. He said that the angel Moroni showed him two golden tablets that contained the life story of Jesus Christ. Smith translated the tablets

Mountain-Man Rendezvous

In the early days, Utah was so isolated that it was hard for the local mountain men to get their goods back to civilization. To solve this problem, U.S. General William Ashley organized an annual rendezvous — a set place and time when mountain men could meet, exchange goods, and socialize. The rendezvous was an instant hit with the mountain men, who lived lonely lives. Rendezvous were soon held all over the state. These events gave the fur traders a chance not just to trade, but also to tell stories, drink, dance, and get news from the outside world.

▼ Visitors climb to the top of ancient Native American cliff dwellings in Forgotten Canyon at Lake Powell.

into English and wrote down the information as *The Book of Mormon*, which was published in 1830. This book gave birth to the Church of Jesus Christ of Latter-day Saints (LDS Church). Church members were called Latter-day Saints, Saints, or Mormons.

The LDS Church grew rapidly, gaining thousands of members over the next decade. Its members formed a close-knit community that rejected outsiders. While these qualities made the Church strong, they also aroused resentment. Non-Mormons, called "Gentiles" by LDS Church members, destroyed church property and attacked church members. To escape persecution, the LDS Church and all its members were forced to move several times.

Matters got even worse when the LDS Church announced its support of polygamy, also called plural marriage. Polygamy allowed male Mormons to have more than one wife at the same time. The U.S. public was outraged, and anti-Mormon sentiment ran high. In 1844, Joseph Smith and his brother Hyrum were thrown into jail on charges that they had destroyed a printing press. Before the brothers could be tried, they were murdered by a Mormon-hating mob that attacked the jail on July 24.

▼ This picture from 1891 shows Salt Lake City as a thriving metropolis rising from the desert landscape.

Heading to the Promised Land

After Smith's death, Brigham Young became the leader of the LDS Church. Young decided to lead the Mormons out of the United States and create a community in a place nobody else wanted. He had heard of the Mexican-owned Salt Lake Valley, which sounded like the perfect location for the new colony.

In 1846, the Mormons left their home (then Nauvoo, Illinois) and headed for the Utah region. On July 24, 1847, an advance party of settlers that included Brigham Young arrived at Salt Lake Valley. "This is the place," Young said when he first glimpsed the dry wasteland. Immediately the Mormons got to work irrigating the land and laying out their new town, which would be called Salt Lake City. They also sent for the rest of the Mormons, who were waiting in Nebraska for the call to join their church leader.

Over the next few years, thousands of Mormons flooded to Salt Lake City. Many of these settlers traveled by foot, pulling their possessions on handcarts across the harsh plains. This period of Mormon history came to be known as the Handcart Migration. The route the people traveled was called the Mormon Trail.

As more and more Mormons arrived in Salt Lake City, the rough Utah landscape became more and more civilized. Irrigation turned the dry ground into farm and grazing land; Salt Lake City grew rapidly. Before long, Brigham Young's paradise was well established. Small groups of Mormons began spreading out from the original city to form new colonies in nearby areas.

Conflict with the United States

While the Mormons were building their desert paradise, important events were taking place on the national scene. One of these events, the signing of the Treaty of Guadalupe Hidalgo in 1848, had particular significance for the Mormons. This treaty ended the Mexican War and gave ownership of the Utah region to the

Brigham Young

Brigham Young was born in Vermont on June 1, 1801. Young converted to Mormonism in 1832. Almost immediately he began his rise in the LDS Church, at first acting as a missionary but earning rapid promotion through the church ranks. By 1841, Young was one of the church's leading officers. He assumed leadership of the church in 1844, after the murder of LDS founder Joseph Smith. A strong and determined leader, Young decided to move the church and all its members across the country to escape persecution. He made the move from 1846 to 1847 and immediately set about transforming the Mormons' new home in Utah's Salt Lake Valley into an agricultural paradise. Over the years, Young became known as a despot who ruled the Mormon community harshly. His methods worked, however. Under Young's leadership, the LDS Church evolved into an effective governing body that focused as much on social and economic as religious issues. Young died on August 29, 1877, leaving behind a thriving church and a lasting legacy.

United States. Once again the LDS Church found itself on U.S. soil.

Resigned to the fact that they could not fight the government forever, the Mormons decided to join it. In 1850, the Mormons asked to be admitted to the Union as the State of Deseret. However, Congress rejected the Mormons' request. Instead it named the region Utah, after the native Utes, and made it into a territory that included present-day Utah and Nevada. (The territory was divided in 1864, when Nevada became a state.) Brigham Young was named governor of the new territory, but his actions were closely supervised by officials sent from Washington.

The Mormons paid little attention to the Washington officials. They ignored the requirements of the U.S. government and continued to practice polygamy. Tension between the Mormons and the United States grew. Finally, in 1857, President James Buchanan sent soldiers to Utah Territory to subdue the Mormons. The result was a series of skirmishes known as the Utah War. The war lasted only until 1858, when Buchanan offered to end hostilities if the Mormons would accept a federally appointed governor and allow U.S. troops to occupy Utah Territory. Brigham Young agreed to the president's terms, and the war ended quietly.

▼ Mormon families often included many children. Large families insured that there were enough hands to work the land and do other chores on early Utah ranches and farms.

Outsiders Arrive

The U.S. troops that arrived following this agreement were the first real threat to the Mormons' treasured isolation. However, they would not be the last. Another blow came in 1861, when the first telegraph line between the east and west coasts of the present-day continental United States was completed in Salt Lake City. An even more important link to the outside world came in 1869, when the nation's first transcontinental railroad was finished. The final spike — made of gold — connecting the eastern and western portions of the railway was driven into the ground at Promontory Point in northern Utah Territory on May 10 of that year.

The late 1860s also brought a flood of prospectors to Utah Territory after gold and silver were found in the mountains. Other minerals such as lead, coal, and copper were soon discovered, resulting in even more mines and miners. The new railway was an essential part of the mining industry. It carried mineral riches away to be sold and brought food and supplies to the territory's expanding worker community.

▲ Railroad workers and officials gather for the driving of the golden spike.

The Road to Statehood

Utah Territory was growing fast. Economically it was ready for statehood. However, the U.S. government would not grant statehood to a territory that allowed polygamy. In fact, it began to actively work against the Mormons' lifestyle. In 1882, Congress passed the Edmunds Act, which imposed heavy fines on polygamists and took away some of their rights. In 1887, even harsher legislation called the Edmunds-Tucker Act was passed. This act stripped the LDS Church of most of its property.

By 1890, the LDS Church president, Wilford Woodruff, was ready to admit defeat. Seeing that he could no longer stand against the U.S. government, Woodruff advised Mormons to abandon the practice of polygamy. He also made other recommendations that pushed Mormons closer to the mainstream of American society. In response to these changes, Congress finally became willing to hear Utah Territory's petition for statehood. On January 4, 1896, Utah became the nation's forty-fifth state.

The Mountain Meadows Massacre

The bloodiest incident of the Utah War occurred on September 11, 1857. A group of about 140 settlers was traveling across the Utah region on the way to California. Suspicious of outsiders, a band of Mormons and Paiute approached the settlers and convinced them to lay down their weapons. As soon as they complied, the Mormons and Paiutes attacked, killing about 120 people. This incident is remembered as the Mountain Meadows Massacre.

The Boom Years

When Utah became a state, its economy was booming. Throughout the late 1800s, new irrigation techniques contributed to the rise of the state's farming and ranching industries. Herds of cattle dotted the land, and wheat, barley, and sugar beets became important crops. At the same time, the mining of gold, silver, copper, lead, and coal continued as Utah's most important industry. Utah's factories, which processed food and mineral products for outside sale, were also essential parts of the state's financial picture.

Utah's economy peaked during the years of U.S. involvement in World War I (1914–1918). During this time, demand for the state's agricultural and factory products was high. Utah's population increased in size and diversity as more and more non-Mormons arrived in the state to join the growing workforce.

Slump and Recovery

The end of World War I brought an end to the surge in demand for Utah's products and badly hurt the state's economy. Things got even worse in 1929, when the Great Depression struck the United States. Mines and factories closed, leaving thousands of Utahns jobless. Then a drought struck in 1931, driving farmers across the state into bankruptcy. By 1933, this run of bad luck had put one-third of all Utahns out of work. Thousands of people left the state in the hope of finding better conditions elsewhere.

Utah's economy received a much-needed boost when the United States entered World War II in 1941. The demand for minerals and agricultural products rose again, putting Utah's fields and mines back to work. Also, with its wide-open spaces and remote location, Utah was the perfect site for military installations. New facilities such as the Dugway Proving Ground, where weapons were tested,

▲ During World War II, B-24 bombers were built on an assembly line at Hill Field near Ogden. These aircraft were an important part of the Allied arsenal that helped win the war.

The Downwinders

In the 1950s and early 1960s, the U.S. government tested nuclear weapons in the Nevada deserts. At that time, southern Utah was considered "virtually uninhabited territory," so bombs were exploded only when the wind blew toward Utah. Utahns who lived within range of the nuclear fallout from government tests became known as "downwinders." Downwinders today are prone to an unusually wide range of ailments, including many forms of cancer.

and Wendover Army Air Base, where air troops trained, kept thousands of Utahns busy with construction and other war-related services.

As the war progressed, Utah's economy moved away from its traditional production base of agriculture and mining and toward a service and industry base. These new industries were mostly located in cities, so people started moving to urban areas. By the 1960s, about 70 percent of Utah's population were city dwellers.

Utah Today

Utah today depends heavily on industry for its economic well-being. It also depends on tourism and recreation and on a growing high-tech community.

As Utah's economy has expanded, so has the state's acceptance into the American mainstream. Distrust of Utah's Mormon population has faded along with the memory of the polygamy years. Today, the Mormons' reputation as a hardworking, optimistic, energetic, and community-minded people remains. They are welcome members of the American cultural landscape.

Utah gained the international spotlight when it hosted the 2002 Winter Olympic Games. Its reputation as a winter sports destination is now worldwide.

The 2002 Winter Olympics

After years of bidding unsuccessfully for the right to host the Winter Olympics, Utah was finally chosen as the site of the 2002 competition. Winning the bid required the construction of many state-of-the-art sports facilities, including a winter sports park near Park City; the E Center, a hockey rink near West Valley City; and the Oquirrh Park speed skating oval in western Salt Lake Valley. Many existing facilities also had to be updated to meet the needs of Olympic competition. Utah officials hope that the many sports sites constructed especially for the Olympics will attract important winter sporting events to the state in future years. They also hope that these facilities will establish Utah as a training site for top-ranked athletes from around the world.

Below: An Olympic racer slides down the luge track during the 2002 Winter Games held near Salt Lake City.

Mormons and More

> Our world is like a giant mosaic made up of many different pieces . . . For the mosaic of mankind, harmony comes only through the tolerance that comes with mutual understanding.
>
> — *Theme of the Dixie International Folkfest, St. George, Utah*

Most of Utah's residents are city dwellers. About 87 percent of the population lives in urban areas; only 13 percent make their homes in rural Utah.

The vast majority of Utah's urban population lives in or near Salt Lake City, the state capital. Salt Lake City itself is the state's largest municipality, and Utah's eight next-largest cities are all within fifty miles of the capital. Many of these cities, including West Valley City, Taylorsville, and Sandy, are essentially suburbs of Salt Lake City. In the busy Salt Lake region, towns bustle and people are everywhere. This region is called the Wasatch Front. It is located along Utah's mountainous Wasatch Range. Much of the rest of the state, however, is a rocky wilderness where few people venture.

Most Utahns trace their ancestry to Europe. English

Age Distribution in Utah
(2000 Census)

0–4	209,378
5–19	601,599
20–24	225,152
25–44	626,600
45–64	380,218
65 & over	190,222

Across One Hundred Years

Utah's three largest foreign-born groups for 1890 and 1990

England 20,899 Denmark 9,023 Sweden 5,986

Mexico 8,922 Canada 5,459 Germany 4,949

Total state population: 207,905
Total foreign-born: 53,064 (25.5%)

Total state population: 1,722,850
Total foreign-born: 58,600 (3.4%)

Patterns of Immigration

The total number of people who immigrated to Utah in 1998 was 3,360. Of that number, the largest immigrant groups were from Mexico (30.8%), Vietnam (4.0%), and China (3.6%).

ancestry is by far the most common. Scandinavian ancestry, including Swedish, Danish, and Norwegian, is the next most common. Other Utahns trace their heritage to Germany, Ireland, Scotland, the Netherlands, France, Wales, and Italy.

Utah's ethnic background is shaped by its dominant religion. The state's Mormon settlers were mostly European, and most Mormon converts today have European roots as well. New Mormons who move to Utah therefore blend into the state's ethnic tapestry.

Minorities

Although most of Utah's residents have European roots, the state does have a growing minority presence. Most notable is Utah's thriving Hispanic community, which makes up about 9 percent of the state's population. Hispanic residents come mostly from Mexico but may trace their ancestry to Central or South American countries.

Next in size is Utah's growing Asian community. Representing 1.7 percent of the state's residents, the diverse Asian population has ties to China, Vietnam, India, Korea, Japan, and other countries in Asia.

Also significant is the state's Native population. In 2000, Utah had 29,684 Native residents (representing 1.3 percent of the population). Many of these residents live on one of the state's eight Indian reservations. The largest of these are the Uintah and Ouray Reservation in the northern

▲ Mormons can trace their ancestry at the Genealogical Society in Salt Lake City. The building contains the histories of hundreds of Mormon families.

DID YOU KNOW?

Utah's Asian community got a huge boost between 1975 and 1990. Twelve thousand refugees from the Vietnam War in Southeast Asia were evacuated to the state.

Heritage and Background, Utah — Year 2000

▶ Here is a look at the racial backgrounds of Utahns today. Utah ranks forty-second among all U.S. states with regard to African Americans as a percentage of the population.

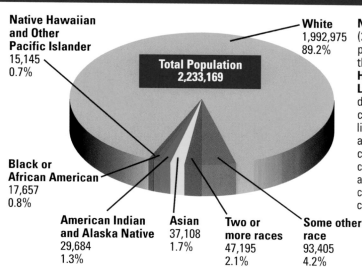

Native Hawaiian and Other Pacific Islander
15,145
0.7%

Total Population 2,233,169

White
1,992,975
89.2%

Black or African American
17,657
0.8%

American Indian and Alaska Native
29,684
1.3%

Asian
37,108
1.7%

Two or more races
47,195
2.1%

Some other race
93,405
4.2%

Note: 9.0% (201,559) of the population identify themselves as **Hispanic** or **Latino,** a cultural designation that crosses racial lines. Hispanics and Latinos are counted in this category as well as the racial category of their choice.

part of the state and the Navajo Reservation, which lies mostly in Arizona and New Mexico but whose northern portion extends into southeast Utah.

Utah's African-American population is small, comprising just 0.8 percent of the state's total population. This is a slight increase from 1990, when African Americans accounted for 0.7 percent of Utah's residents.

Religion

Utah's religious community is dominated by the Church of Jesus Christ of Latter-day Saints. About 70 percent of Utah's residents (roughly 1.6 million people) are Mormon. The worldwide center of the Mormon religion is Salt Lake City, which contains the massive Salt Lake Temple. Completed in 1893, the temple is the central information point for about 11 million Mormons worldwide. Also

Educational Levels of Utah Workers (age 25 and over)	
Less than 9th grade	38,426
9th to 12th grade, no diploma	108,585
High school graduate, including equivalency	294,426
Some college, no degree or associate degree	443,492
Bachelor's degree	213,959
Graduate or professional degree	99,004

▼ The Salt Lake City skyline extends to the shore of the Great Salt Lake.

important is the nearby Mormon Tabernacle, a meeting place and the home of the world-famous Mormon Tabernacle Choir.

Although they have less impact, other religions have also found a home in Utah. There are more than sixty established religious groups practicing in the state today. The largest non-Mormon denomination is Roman Catholicism, followed by Protestantism. All other major religions, including Judaism, Buddhism, and Islam, are practiced in Utah, though in much smaller numbers.

Education

Mormon schools have existed in Utah since the original settlers arrived in 1847. However, public schooling was not established until 1890, when Utah passed a law creating and funding free elementary schools. Public high schools were created by Utah's state constitution in 1895.

Today, Utah has about eight hundred public elementary and secondary schools with an enrollment of approximately 500,000 students. The public school system is excellent, thanks to the founding Mormons' belief in the importance of education. Utah ranks high in its percentage of both high school and college graduates, and the statewide literacy rate is 94 percent. These good results are achieved despite cramped conditions in the schools. Utah has an unusually large proportion of school-age children. Also, the state is growing fast — Utah's population change of 29.6 percent between 1990 and 2000 ranks it the fourth-fastest-growing U.S. state. For these reasons, many Utah school districts have found in recent years that they have more students than space.

In addition to its elementary and secondary schools, Utah also runs ten public colleges and universities. Major state-run schools include the University of Utah in Salt Lake City (enrollment 27,500) and Utah State University in Logan (enrollment 17,000). The state's private colleges include Brigham Young University in Provo and Westminster College in Salt Lake City.

Baby Boom

Utah has by far the highest birthrate in the United States. In 2000, 21.9 children were born for every one thousand Utah residents. The state with the next highest birthrate was Texas, where 17.8 children were born for every one thousand residents. Utah's high birthrate is usually attributed to its overwhelmingly Mormon population. The LDS Church encourages large families, so church members are likely to have more children than the average U.S. resident.

Mountains and Deserts

> Wherever we look there is but a wilderness of rocks —
> deep gorges where the rivers are lost below cliffs
> and towers and pinnacles, and ten thousand strangely
> carved forms in every direction, and beyond them
> mountains blending with the clouds.
>
> — *John Wesley Powell*, Diary of Colorado River Explorations, *1869*

With a land area of 82,144 square miles (212,753 sq km), Utah is the twelfth-largest U.S. state. It is shaped like a rectangle with a smaller rectangular chunk taken out of the northeastern corner. Utah is bordered by Idaho and Wyoming to the north, Arizona to the south, Colorado to the east, and Nevada to the west. The southeastern tip of Utah touches the corners of Colorado, New Mexico, and Arizona — the only place in the United States where four states meet.

Land elevations in Utah range from a high of 13,528 feet (4,123 m) at Kings Peak in the Uinta Mountains of the northeast to a low of 2,350 feet (716 m) at Beaver Dam Wash near St. George in the southwest.

Utah's Regions
Utah is divided into three main geographic regions. The Colorado Plateau is in the southeast, the Basin and Range Province is in the west, and the Middle Rocky Mountain

Highest Point
Kings Peak
13,528 feet (4,123 m)
above sea level

▼ *From left to right*: Monument Valley; a coyote; the Four Corners Marker; birch trees in winter; the Great Salt Lake; Mount Timpanogos.

Province is in the north-central and northeast regions.

The Colorado Plateau is a desert region where ridges, mesas, fins, buttes, natural arches, and other rock formations dot the land. These formations are made of pink, white, red, brown, and yellow sandstone. The Colorado Plateau is also crisscrossed by deep gorges and canyons. The deepest canyons are found along the Colorado and Green Rivers.

The Basin and Range Province is an area of mountain ranges separated by broad valleys. In this barren region, little rain falls and few plants grow. The Basin and Range Province contains several deserts, including the Great Salt Lake Desert in the northwest, the Sevier Desert in the midregion, and the Escalante Desert in the southwest.

The Middle Rocky Mountain Province is part of the Rocky Mountains, which run all the way down the midsection of the United States. This is Utah's hilliest region and the home of the state's highest elevations. The two Rocky Mountain ranges in Utah are the Wasatch Range, which runs north to south down the middle of the state, and the Uinta Range, which runs west to east across the northeastern part of the state.

Utah's climate varies by region. Hot, dry, desert conditions are typical in many parts of the Basin and Range Province and the Colorado Plateau. Mountainous regions are much cooler and wetter, receiving plenty of rain in the warm months and lots of snow in the wintertime.

Rivers and Lakes

One of Utah's most important geological features is the Great Salt Lake. Lying in the northwestern part of the state, this body of water is the largest saltwater lake in the Western Hemisphere. The lake is salty because rivers only run into it,

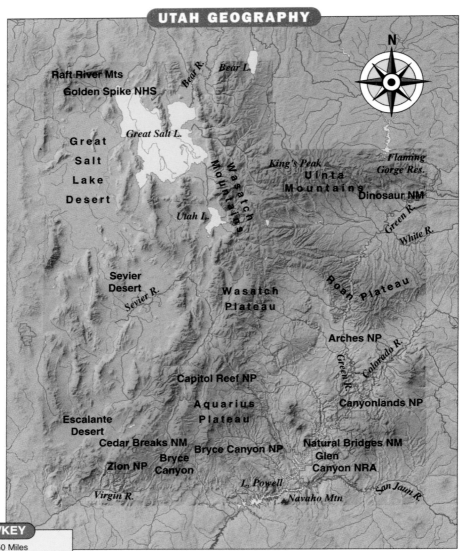

UTAH GEOGRAPHY

Raft River Mts
Golden Spike NHS

Bear R.

Bear L.

N

Great
Salt
Lake
Desert

Great Salt L.

King's Peak

*Flaming
Gorge Res.*

Uinta
Mountains

Dinosaur NM

Wasatch Mountains

Green R.

White R.

Utah L.

Sevier
Desert

Sevier R.

Wasatch
Plateau

Roan Plateau

Arches NP

Green R.

Colorado R.

Capitol Reef NP

Aquarius
Plateau

Canyonlands NP

Escalante
Desert

Cedar Breaks NM

Zion NP

Bryce
Canyon

Bryce Canyon NP

Natural Bridges NM
Glen
Canyon NRA

Virgin R.

L. Powell

Navaho Mtn

San Juan R.

not out. The inflowing rivers carry salty minerals that become trapped in the lake's vast basin.

All of Utah's other large lakes contain fresh water. Natural freshwater lakes include Utah Lake near Provo and Bear Lake on the state's northern border. Lake Powell in the southeast is an artificial lake, created by the backup of the Colorado River behind Arizona's Glen Canyon Dam.

Utah has several major rivers. The longest is the Colorado, which crosses the southeast corner of the state. Next is the Green River, a major tributary of the Colorado that flows down the eastern side of Utah and joins the Colorado in Canyonlands National Park. A third major river is the Sevier, which forms a great loop in southwestern Utah before draining into the mostly dry Sevier Lake bed.

Plants and Animals

About 30 percent of Utah's land area is covered with forests. The state's forest areas are concentrated in the Middle Rocky Mountain Province. In this region, tall trees such as ponderosa pines, sycamores, and quaking aspens blanket the land. A huge variety of flowers and grasses also grows in this area.

Utah's deserts, too, host plant life, but of a very different type. Short shrubs and stunted trees are common in Utah's dry areas. Cactuses, sego lilies, yucca plants, and tough grasses are part of the desert landscape.

Both forests and deserts are home to a wide variety of mammals. Large mammals such as cougars, black bears, and mountain goats roam the state's mountains. Antelope, elks, moose, and other deerlike animals can also be found in forested areas, as can otters, weasels, and other small mammals. Coyotes prowl dry areas of the state. Lizards, snakes, and scorpions are also common in Utah's deserts, as are prairie dogs, jackrabbits, mice, and other small creatures.

Many types of birds and fish are found in Utah. Great Salt Lake is an especially good place to see birds. Enormous numbers of birds often settle around the lake, which is a common rest stop for migrating flocks. Fish are common throughout the state. Bass, perch, trout, and other types are plentiful in most of Utah's rivers and streams.

Major Rivers

Colorado River
1,450 miles (2,333 km)

Green River
730 miles (1,175 km)

Sevier River
280 miles (451 km)

DID YOU KNOW?

An earthquake zone called the Wasatch Fault runs along the western edge of the Wasatch Range. Scientists believe that a major earthquake occurs along this fault every few hundred years. However, no big earthquake has hit Utah in the last 400 years.

▼ The Colorado River has cut deep canyons through southeastern Utah.

A Hive of Industry

> We . . . enjoyed the pleasant strangeness of a city of fifteen thousand inhabitants with no loafers perceptible in it. . . . Everywhere were workshops, factories, and all manner of industries; and intent faces and busy hands were to be seen wherever one looked.
>
> — *Author Mark Twain*, Roughing It, *1872, writing about Salt Lake City*

Utah was envisioned by its Mormon settlers as an agricultural paradise. In the early years, the state was just that as settlers planted crops and established herds of cattle. Utah's agricultural industry was not only the keystone of the economy, it was also a matter of survival to the people who worked on and lived off the land.

Mining, too, was an essential part of Utah's early economy. Income from the sale of gold, silver, lead, coal, and copper supported Utah and encouraged a growing population.

Today, a shift has taken place. Mining and agriculture, once so important, now make up just a small percentage of Utah's gross state product (the total value of goods and services produced in the state). Service industries — those in which services, not actual goods, are sold — are now the mainstay of Utah's economy.

Services

Utah's important services include finance, insurance, and real estate; wholesale and retail sales; and transportation, communication, and utilities. In 2000, these services accounted for 43.4 percent of Utah's gross state product. Small businesses, especially those providing information technology, also contribute to Utah's economy.

Utah's government workers comprise part of the services sector as well, accounting for 14.1 percent of the gross state product in 2000. Utah's federal, state, local, and military

Top Employers (of workers age sixteen and over)	
Services	41.0%
Wholesale and retail trade	16.3%
Manufacturing	12.1%
Construction	8.2%
Transportation, communications, and public utilities	8.2%
Finance, insurance, and real estate	6.8%
Federal, state, and local government (including military)	5.5%
Agriculture, forestry, fisheries, and mining	1.9%

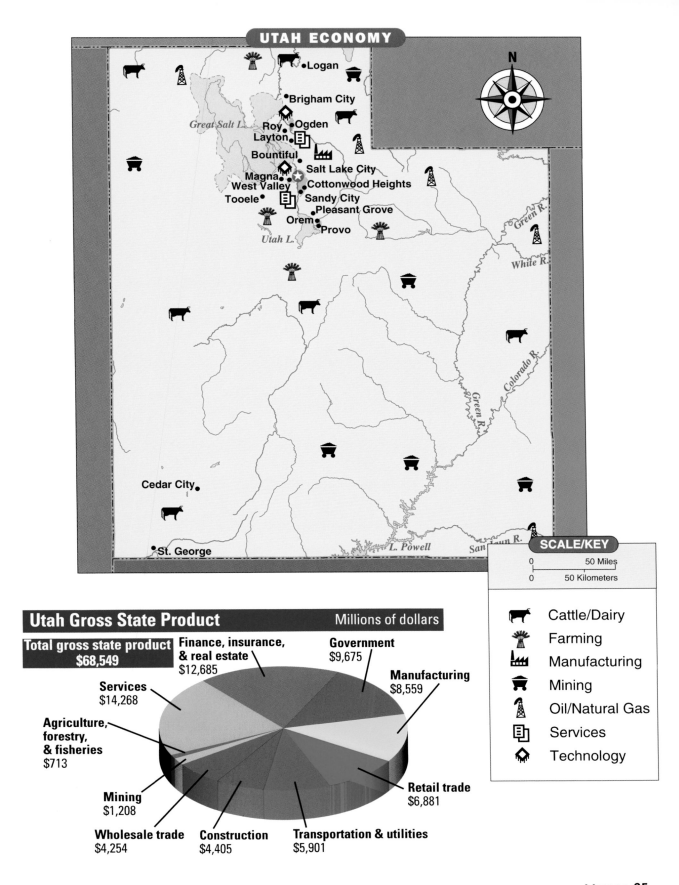

N

Logan

Brigham City

Great Salt L.

Roy • Ogden
Layton

Bountiful

Magna • Salt Lake City
West Valley • Cottonwood Heights
Tooele • Sandy City
Pleasant Grove
Orem • Provo
Utah L.

Green R.

White R.

Colorado R.

Green R.

Cedar City

L. Powell
San Juan R.

St. George

SCALE/KEY

| 0 | 50 Miles |
| 0 | 50 Kilometers |

🐂 Cattle/Dairy
🌾 Farming
🏭 Manufacturing
⛏ Mining
🛢 Oil/Natural Gas
🗐 Services
◈ Technology

Utah Gross State Product
Millions of dollars

Total gross state product $68,549

Finance, insurance, & real estate $12,685

Government $9,675

Manufacturing $8,559

Services $14,268

Agriculture, forestry, & fisheries $713

Mining $1,208

Wholesale trade $4,254

Construction $4,405

Transportation & utilities $5,901

Retail trade $6,881

workers are part of this government sector, as are the state's public schoolteachers.

Tourism is another important service industry in Utah. Visitors to Utah's national parks, recreation areas, and other attractions contribute about $3.7 billion to the state's economy each year.

Manufacturing

After services, manufacturing is the next most important sector of Utah's economy. Manufacturing activities contributed 12.5 percent of the gross state product in 2000. The state's main durable products (those meant to last three years or more) include medical instruments, electronic equipment and instruments, primary and fabricated metals, and motor vehicles and other transportation equipment. The manufacture of industrial machinery is also important.

Utah's main nondurable products (those meant to last fewer than three years) are food products, chemicals, and petroleum products.

Agriculture and Mining

In 2000, mining was responsible for 1.8 percent of Utah's gross state product. Oil and natural gas are the state's most important mining products. Coal mining is next in importance, followed closely by metals, including copper, gold, silver, lead, nickel, zinc, magnesium, and others.

Agriculture, forestry, and fisheries today are the smallest sector of Utah's economy. Together, these

The First Department Store

Zions Cooperative Mercantile Institution (ZCMI) in Salt Lake City has been called "America's first department store." Founded by Brigham Young in 1868, the ZCMI ensured Mormons that goods would be sold to them at reasonable prices. (Prices became inflated as non-Mormons moved to the area.) ZCMI's mission was to sell goods "as low as they can possibly be sold, and let the profits be divided among the people at large." ZCMI was an instant success when it was created and still exists today, with branches in several suburban malls.

industries contributed just one percent of Utah's gross state product in 2000. Most of this income comes from the state's 15,500 farms. Livestock, including beef cattle, sheep, and hogs, is responsible for about three-quarters of the state's agricultural income; chicken farming is a smaller but growing part of the livestock picture. The remaining one-quarter of Utah's agricultural income comes from crops, the most important of which are hay, corn, wheat, and barley.

▲ The Bingham Canyon Mine is one-half-mile deep and two-and-a-half miles wide.

Transportation and Communication

Utah is no longer an isolated desert. Various land and air routes connect it to other states and allow for international travel. The state is crisscrossed by roads, the largest of which are the interstate highways. I-15 is the state's major north-south route, and I-80 is the major east-west route. Many smaller roads bring residents and visitors to the area's isolated towns and attractions. A number of railway lines bring cargo into, out of, and across Utah, and the state is easily reached via Salt Lake City International Airport, which was the country's twenty-sixth busiest airport in 2000.

Within Utah, a well-developed communications network keeps residents in touch. The state has about one hundred radio stations that broadcast everything from news to country music, from oldies to rock. Sixteen TV stations carry news and entertainment programs. The state also has nearly sixty newspapers. Of these, seven are published daily. The state's oldest daily newspaper is the *Deseret News*, first published in 1850. The largest paper is *The Salt Lake Tribune*, with a daily circulation of about 135,000. These publications and others keep Utahns informed about what is going on in their state and around the world.

DID YOU KNOW?

The town of Kanab is the center of a small but thriving Utah film industry. It is sometimes called "Utah's Little Hollywood" because so many Western movies have been filmed there over the years.

Made in Utah

Leading farm products and crops
Beef cattle and calves
Sheep and lambs
Corn
Wheat
Hay
Hogs

Other products
Medical instruments
Electronic equipment
Food products
Primary and
   fabricated metals
Transportation
   equipment
Coal, oil, and
   natural gas

Major Airports		
Airport	**Location**	**Passengers per year (2000)**
Salt Lake City International	Salt Lake City	19,900,810

Daily Operations

> Be it enacted by the Senate and House of Representatives of the United States of America in Congress assembled, That the inhabitants of all that part of the area of the United States now constituting the Territory of Utah, as at present described, may become the State of Utah . . .
>
> — *Utah Enabling Act, July 16, 1894*

Utah has had only one constitution in its state history. The constitution was adopted in 1896, when Utah became a state. This document contains some unusual religious restrictions that were meant to satisfy the federal government at a time when anti-Mormon sentiments were running high. Besides providing for the separation of church and state, the constitution specifies that no particular church shall "dominate the State or interfere with its functions." It also specifies that "polygamous or plural marriages are forever prohibited."

The system of government in Utah — just like that of the U.S. federal government — is divided into three branches: executive, legislative, and judicial. The executive branch administers laws, the legislative branch makes laws, and the judicial branch interprets and enforces laws.

The Executive Branch

The executive branch includes the governor, lieutenant governor, auditor, treasurer, and attorney general. Each of these officials is elected to a four-year term of office. Elected executive-branch officials may serve no more than three consecutive terms. The governor and other executive branch officers oversee more than thirty state agencies, including the Departments of Agriculture and Food, Commerce, Health, and Transportation.

The governor serves as Utah's chief executive officer.

Elected Posts in the Executive Branch		
Office	Length of Term	Term Limits
Governor	4 years	3 consecutive terms
Lieutenant Governor	4 years	3 consecutive terms
Auditor	4 years	3 consecutive terms
Treasurer	4 years	3 consecutive terms
Attorney General	4 years	3 consecutive terms

DID YOU KNOW?
Utah's Jake Garn, U.S. senator from 1974 to 1992, was the first Congressperson in space. In April 1985, Garn circled Earth 108 times in the space shuttle *Discovery*.

The governor's main duty is reviewing and either approving or vetoing (rejecting) all proposed laws, which are called bills. If the governor vetoes a bill, it can still become a law if at least two-thirds of the members in each legislative division overrule the veto.

The Legislative Branch

Utah's legislative branch is called the Utah Legislature. It includes the senate, with twenty-nine members, and the house of representatives, with seventy-five members. Senators serve four-year terms, while representatives serve two-year terms. Senators may serve no more than three consecutive terms, and representatives may serve no more than six consecutive terms.

The state legislature meets in Salt Lake City, Utah's capital, each year for forty-five days. The governor may call special sessions at other times if they are needed. During a legislative session, senators and representatives work to create new laws.

▼ A statue of Chief Massasoit, a friend of the Pilgrims who first landed in what is now Massachusetts, stands in front of Utah's capitol building. Utah sculptor Cyrus Dallin created this statue as well as an identical one in Plymouth, Massachusetts.

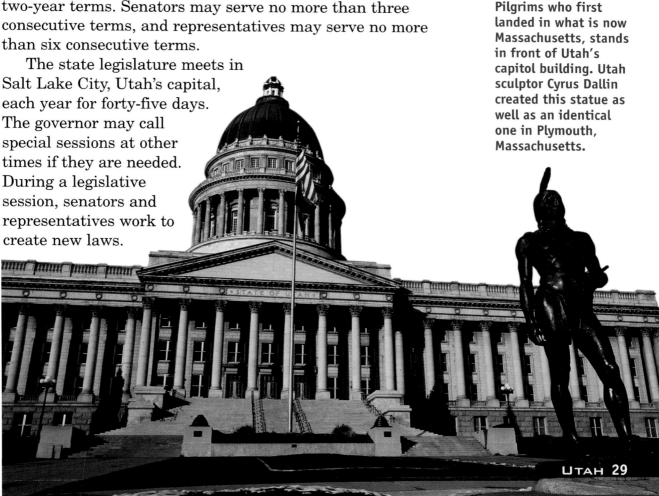

Laws start out as bills that must be voted on by both the house and the senate. If a bill is passed by both bodies, it is given to the governor for approval or veto.

The Judicial Branch

The main job of the judicial branch is to interpret laws. This work is done by courts and judges in a many-leveled system, in which higher courts oversee the work of lower courts. In Utah, the highest court is called the supreme court. The supreme court reviews the rulings of the state's lower courts when necessary. It has five justices who are elected to ten-year renewable terms. The justices elect a chief justice by majority vote to serve for four years, and an associate chief justice to serve for two years.

Directly under the supreme court is the court of appeals, which has seven judges who serve six-year terms. The court of appeals reviews the decisions of lower courts and may decide to pass them on to the supreme court.

Under the court of appeals are the district courts. Utah has eight district courts with seventy judges, all of whom are elected to six-year terms.

The lowest level of Utah's judicial system includes circuit courts, juvenile courts, justices of the peace, and special courts that handle smaller cases.

Local Government

At the local level, Utah is split into twenty-nine counties. Each county is responsible for its own administration, law enforcement, finances, elections, and other local matters. Cache County in northern Utah is run by an elected executive and part-time council members. Most of Utah's other counties are governed by teams of three commissioners who are elected to four-year terms.

National Representation

Like all U.S. states, Utah has two members in the U.S. Senate. It has three members in the House of

Legislature			
House	Number of Members	Length of Term	Term Limits
Senate	29 senators	4 years	3 consecutive terms
House of Representatives	75 representatives	2 years	6 consecutive terms

Representatives. U.S. senators are elected to six-year terms; representatives are elected to two-year terms.

In 1994, Utah passed a law that will impose term limits of twelve years on its federal legislators starting in 2006. However, a similar law passed by the state of Oregon was found unconstitutional by the U.S. Supreme Court in 2001, so it is possible that Utah's law will be challenged before it takes effect.

State Politics

Utahns tend to be conservative. They voted for Republican presidential candidates in all but two elections during the twentieth century. In 2000, Republican presidential candidate George W. Bush earned 67 percent of the state's votes, trouncing Democratic candidate Al Gore. Historically, a slight majority of Utah's federal senators and representatives have also been Republicans.

▼ Utah's constitution is displayed in Salt Lake City, the state capital.

Orrin Hatch: The Musical Senator

Orrin Grant Hatch was born on March 22, 1934, in Pittsburgh, Pennsylvania. He attended Brigham Young University and law school at the University of Pittsburgh, before moving to Salt Lake City to open a law firm. In 1976, Hatch was elected to the U.S. Senate on the Republican ticket and has retained his seat through the present day. Hatch is known for his conservative attitudes on abortion, capital punishment, and school prayer. However, he also has a habit of bewildering his Republican supporters by taking liberal stances on other issues, including day care and health insurance. In addition to his work in the U.S. Senate, Hatch is also a songwriter. A devout Mormon, Hatch has written hundreds of hymns and patriotic and gospel songs, many of which have been recorded by famous artists.

Arts, History, and Outdoors

> Recreation and diversion are as necessary to our well-being as the most serious pursuits of life. If you wish to dance, dance, and you are just as prepared for prayer meeting as you were before.
>
> — *Brigham Young as quoted in* Dancing as an Aspect of Early Mormon and Utah Culture *by Leona Holbrook*

Utah residents have diverse interests, ranging from the arts to the outdoors, from history to sports. The state has a wide variety of cultural and lifestyle offerings that reflect the interests of its residents.

Salt Lake City is Utah's undisputed cultural center. The capital and its surrounding communities offer most of the state's fine and performing arts as well as professional sporting events. Utah's unique historic and outdoor attractions are scattered throughout the Salt Lake area and the rest of the state.

Performing Arts

A number of fine musical groups call Utah home. The state's most famous musical organization is the Mormon Tabernacle Choir. Established in 1847, this 320-voice ensemble is based in Salt Lake City and enjoys worldwide fame. The Choir gives choral concerts locally, nationally, and internationally. Its rehearsals are open to the public. Other popular Salt Lake-based musical groups include the Utah Opera Company and the Utah Symphony Orchestra, whose performances draw half a million attendees each year.

DID YOU KNOW?

Moab is sometimes called the "mountain biking capital of the world." The town's Slickrock Bicycle Trail, which passes over petrified sand dunes, is a favorite destination for cyclists.

▼ This is the Place Monument, south of Old Deseret Village, commemorating the arrival of Mormon Pioneers to the Salt Lake Valley in 1847.

Salt Lake City also provides entertainment for dance fans. Well-known groups include Ballet West, a traditional dance troupe, and the Repertory Dance Theatre, a modern dance company.

People who love the dramatic arts have a variety of entertainment options as well. The Pioneer Theatre Company and the Salt Lake Acting Company, both in Salt Lake City, stage multiple productions annually. In the southwestern corner of the state, the yearly Shakespearean Utah Festival in Cedar City is another popular event. The Sundance Film Festival, an independent-film showcase organized by actor and director Robert Redford, takes over the town of Park City for ten days each year.

Museums

Utah boasts many fine museums. The University of Utah campus in Salt Lake City is the home of two of the state's most popular venues — the Utah Museum of Natural History, which has exhibits about geology, biology, and Native history, and the Utah Museum of Fine Arts, which features exhibits from ancient Egyptian to modern American visual arts.

Another popular museum is located on the Brigham Young University campus in Provo. The university's

The Tabernacle Organ

The internationally famous Mormon Tabernacle Choir is often accompanied by the Tabernacle Organ, one of the world's most remarkable musical instruments. The organ has 11,623 pipes and five separate keyboards. Today the organ is powered by electricity, but when it was first built it was powered by four men pumping air bellows. The Church of Jesus Christ of Latter-day Saints designed this magnificent organ to symbolize the church's belief in worshiping God through music.

Museum of Art hosts major traveling exhibits and displays an extensive permanent collection as well. The nearby Springville Museum of Art is also considered one of the finest in the state.

Historic Attractions

Many of Utah's more popular tourist attractions celebrate the state's past. Dinosaurs, the area's most ancient residents, are on display at Dinosaur National Monument in the northeastern part of the state. Paleontologists consider this site to be America's most important natural display of fossilized dinosaur bones. Meanwhile, the history of Utah's first human residents can be explored at Anasazi State Park, which contains the preserved remains of an ancient village. The Trail of the Ancients in the southeast is another interesting attraction. This marked automobile trail leads visitors to a variety of Ancestral Puebloan sites.

Utah's Mormon heritage is an integral part of the state's history. This heritage is on display at Utah's most visited attraction: Temple Square in Salt Lake City. Salt Lake Temple, which was built by Utah's original Mormon settlers, and the egg-shaped Mormon Tabernacle are the main attractions here. Nearby, This Is the Place State

▲ The Visitors Center at Dinosaur National Monument in Jensen, Utah, houses the fossilized bones of creatures that lived 150 million years ago. Visitors can view a sandstone wall with more than 2,000 exposed dinosaur bones.

DID YOU KNOW?

Between 1935 and 1970, the Bonneville Salt Flats dominated the world of high-speed motor sports. Nearly every speed record set during this period was reached at Bonneville. On October 23, 1970, Gary Gabelich reached a speed of 622.407 miles per hour in a rocket-powered vehicle called the *Blue Flame*.

Heritage Park also celebrates Utah's first non-Native settlers. The park includes a re-created frontier town where "pioneers" demonstrate traditional crafts and skills. The Beehive and Lion houses are yet other interesting sites. Beehive House was Founding Father Brigham Young's house; the adjoining Lion House was the home of Young's twenty-plus wives and their children.

Other historic attractions of note include the Mountain Meadows Massacre Historic Site near St. George, the Golden Spike National Historic Site at Promontory Point, and the mining ghost towns of Ophir, Eureka, and Gold Hill.

The Great Outdoors

Utah's spectacular scenery makes this state's national parks a major draw. Millions of visitors each year enjoy the natural arches, ridges, and other formations in Zion National Park, Bryce Canyon National Park, Arches National Park, Capitol Reef National Park, and others. Incredible views are also on display at the Grand Staircase-Escalante National Monument, one of the world's wildest deserts. Colorful rock formations, narrow canyons, rivers, and waterfalls are the

DID YOU KNOW?

Rainbow Bridge National Monument on the banks of Lake Powell is the world's largest natural rock span. It is 278 feet (84.7 m) wide and 309 feet (94.2 m) high.

▼ The Grand Staircase-Escalante National Monument was one of the last areas of the United States to be explored and mapped. Its rugged terrain and spectacular rock formations make this area popular with backcountry explorers.

main features of this 1.9-million-acre (768,930 ha) wilderness area.

With many rivers and streams, thick forests, abundant wildlife, and rugged terrain, Utah's Rocky Mountain region is a paradise for those who love to be outdoors and active. Popular summer activities in the Rockies include hiking, fishing, camping, and whitewater rafting. Utah residents and visitors also enjoy the recreational opportunities offered by Lake Powell, Utah Lake, and other area reservoirs.

In winter, residents turn their thoughts to downhill and cross-country skiing at one of Utah's world-class resorts. Park City, Deer Valley, Snowbird, and The Canyons are a few of the ski areas that not only draw locals but also tourists from around the world.

The Sports Scene

Utah sports fans root for many teams. Utah's best-known franchise is the Jazz, a National Basketball Association (NBA) team. Athletes such as Karl Malone and John Stockton dazzle fans in the Delta Center, the Jazz's home arena. Other professional sports teams are the Women's National Basketball Association's Starzz, the World Indoor Soccer League's Freezz, the International

Sport	Team	Home
Basketball	Utah Jazz	Delta Center, Salt Lake City
Basketball	Utah Starzz	Delta Center, Salt Lake City

Ski Utah

Utah's license plates read "Ski Utah! The Greatest Snow on Earth." Few skiers would disagree with this claim. Snow conditions at resorts such as Park City, Deer Valley, and The Canyons are among the best in the world. As an added bonus, ski slopes are not nearly as crowded in Utah as they are in nearby Colorado. This is probably because Colorado offers more nightlife than laid-back Utah. But for the ski fanatic who wants to make as many runs as possible every day and does not mind a limited choice of post-ski activities, Utah is definitely the place to be.

Hockey League's Grizzlies, and the baseball minor league Salt Lake Stingers.

Utah's colleges also provide sports entertainment. Utah residents get especially excited about the annual University of Utah versus Brigham Young University (BYU) football game. BYU is a nationally ranked football powerhouse with fans who live all over the U.S. and not just in Utah.

Racing fans get their thrills at the Bonneville Speedway on the Bonneville Salt Flats. Events there allow both professional and amateur racers to zoom at top speed across the world's hardest, flattest ground.

Utah's biggest sporting moment came when it hosted the 2002 Winter Olympic Games. The Games were not only an international spectacle, but also a huge moneymaker. An estimated fifty thousand visitors per day poured a total of $4.8 billion into Utah's economy during the Games. Utah tourism officials hope that exposure from the 2002 Winter Olympics will increase the popularity of its ski areas and make them even more inviting to vacationers.

Utah Greats

Born on August 21, 1959, in New Jersey, Jim McMahon moved to Utah during his sophomore year of high school. He attended BYU, where he was the football team's star quarterback. In 1982, he signed with the National Football League's Chicago Bears. For the next several years, McMahon was the Bears' most outstanding player. In 1986, he led the team to its first-ever Super Bowl victory.

Karl Malone's nickname is "The Mailman" because he always delivers. Malone is the six foot, nine inch (2 m) power forward for the Utah Jazz basketball team. A thirteen-time All Star, and twice Most Valuable Player, he was also a member of the 1992 Olympic gold medal basketball "Dream Team." He founded the Karl Malone Foundation to help kids and families and is active in the Utah Special Olympics. He was presented the 1998 Henry P. Iba Citizen Athlete Award for his work in the community.

▼ **Utah Jazz power forward Karl Malone pulls down a rebound against the Los Angeles Clippers.**

Great Utahns

Those who have made Utah their home . . . have possessed
the courageous spirit of true pioneers.
— *Authors Tom and Gayen Wharton*, Utah, *2001*

Following are only a few of the thousands of people who were born, died, or spent much of their lives in
Utah and made extraordinary contributions to the state and the nation.

JAMES (JIM) BECKWOURTH
MOUNTAIN MAN

BORN: *April 26, 1798, Fredericksburg, VA*
DIED: *September 25, 1866, Denver, CO*

Jim Beckwourth was one of Utah's best-known mountain men. The son of a white plantation owner and an African-American slave, Beckwourth had a reputation for telling outlandish stories with himself as the hero. Several different times, his thirst for adventure led him to live with Utah's Native tribes. One of his stories claimed that he became a Crow chief who led the tribe in a war against its Blackfoot enemies. His stories were recorded in the 1856 book *The Life and Adventures of James P. Beckwourth.*

JEDEDIAH SMITH
FUR TRADER

BORN: *June 24, 1798, Bainbridge, NY*
DIED: *May 27, 1831, unknown, NM*

Fur trader Jedediah Smith is best remembered for his legendary explorations. He was the first non-Native to cross Utah both from west to east and from north to south. The records Smith kept of his travels paved the way for future expeditions. In his time, Smith was considered an unusual man because he did not smoke, drink, swear, or chase women — common activities for Utah's mountain men.

JIM BRIDGER
SCOUT

BORN: *March 17, 1804, Richmond, VA*
DIED: *July 17, 1881, near Kansas City, MO*

At the age of eighteen, Jim Bridger signed up with a fur-trapping venture based in Missouri. He was soon roaming the unknown West, including the territory that would become Utah, in search of game. Bridger was probably the first non-Native person to see Utah's Great Salt Lake. By the mid-1800s, Bridger was so familiar with Utah and the surrounding areas that he entered government service as a scout. Making use of his exceptional language and tracking skills, Bridger safely led many expeditions through the rugged Utah wilderness.

WAKARA
UTE CHIEF

BORN: *about 1815, near the Spanish Fork River*
DIED: *January 28, 1855, Chicken Creek*

As a young man, Wakara (nicknamed "Walker" by white men) quickly learned Spanish and English and became his tribe's main contact with settlers entering the Utah region. He later became a Ute chief, earning wealth for his people by trading with the settlers. He also participated in the Mexican slave trade, which involved kidnapping members of other Native tribes and selling them as slaves in Mexico. Wakara was friendly to the Mormons when they first arrived in Utah but changed his attitude when they occupied Ute land and tried to disrupt Wakara's profitable slave trade. Growing tension resulted in the Walker War of 1853–1854, a series of skirmishes in which a small number of both settlers and Utes were killed.

BLACK HAWK
UTE CHIEF

BORN: *around 1840, place unknown*
DIED: *1870, Santaquin*

Black Hawk is known for a war that was named after him. This Native warrior led the Utes against the Mormons in a Black Hawk War. (a more famous Blackhawk War took place in Illinois in 1832.) Black Hawk's war parties mostly stole Mormon cattle, but settlers were sometimes killed. The raids were made in an attempt to gather food for the Utes after the harsh winter of 1864.

ROBERT LEROY PARKER
OUTLAW

BORN: *April 15, 1866, Circleville*
DIED: *1910, Bolivia, South America*

Robert Leroy Parker is better known as Butch Cassidy, infamous outlaw of the Old West. Born to strict Mormon parents, Cassidy learned the art of cattle rustling (stealing) at a young age from one of his father's farmhands. Soon Cassidy got involved with Colorado's McCarty Gang and expanded his criminal activities to include robbing trains and banks. After spending time in jail for cattle rustling, Cassidy joined up with the Hole-in-the-Wall Gang, also known as the Wild Bunch. This group was responsible for about a dozen train and bank robberies in Wyoming, Colorado, and Utah between 1896 and 1901. Pursued by the law, Cassidy and his sidekick, the Sundance Kid (whose real name was Harry Longabaugh), eventually fled to Bolivia.

No one is certain where or how they died, but most historians believe they were killed in a shootout with Bolivian law enforcement agents about 1910.

WILLIAM "BIG BILL" HAYWOOD
LABOR LEADER

BORN: *February 4, 1869, Salt Lake City*
DIED: *May 18, 1928, Russia*

Utah native "Big Bill" Haywood was one of the nation's most notorious labor leaders. At age fifteen, Haywood became a miner. Later he joined the Western Federation of Miners labor union and helped to found the Industrial Workers of the World (IWW). Haywood earned a reputation for being aggressive and encouraging union members to commit acts of violence. In 1917, Haywood and other IWW leaders were arrested for sedition (provoking unlawful acts). To avoid jail, Haywood fled to Russia, where he lived until his death in 1928.

MAHONRI YOUNG
ARTIST

BORN: *August 9, 1877, Salt Lake City*
DIED: *November 2, 1957, New York, NY*

Mahonri Young was the grandson of Brigham Young, the Mormon leader who settled Utah. He studied art throughout his life and became increasingly well-known as the years went by. Although he worked in many media, Young is best known for his sculptures. Two large sculptures by Young, *Sea Gull Monument* and *This Is the Place Monument*, stand today in Utah. Young's art is also on display at the Metropolitan Museum of Art, the Whitney Museum of American Art, and other prestigious institutions.

J. WILLARD MARRIOTT
BUSINESS OWNER

BORN: *September 17, 1900, Marriott Settlement*
DIED: *August 13, 1985, Wolfeboro, NH*

Utah native J. Willard Marriott was the founder of the Marriott hotel chain. After growing up in a Utah ranching family, Marriott turned to education and entrepreneurship as a way out of poverty. He opened his first business, an A&W Root Beer stand, in 1927. Over the years, Marriott's food-service empire grew. In 1957, he decided to expand the business into other areas, and the first Marriott hotel was opened. Many more followed. By the time Marriott died in 1985, the Marriott Corporation had become a powerful organization that controlled 125 hotels, 667 restaurants, 935 franchises, 3 cruise ships, and more.

LORETTA YOUNG
ACTRESS

BORN: *January 6, 1913, Salt Lake City*
DIED: *August 12, 2000, Los Angeles, CA*

Loretta Young was born in Salt Lake City but moved to Los Angeles with her mother and siblings as a young girl.

She began appearing in films at age four and got her first real break in 1927, when she landed a big role in the film *Naughty But Nice*. She later starred in films opposite Clark Gable, Cary Grant, Gary Cooper, and other leading men. Young won an Academy Award for her role in the 1947 movie *The Farmer's Daughter*. In 1953, she became the first star to break into television with the *Loretta*

Young Show. The show ran for eight years and earned her three Emmy awards.

NOLAN KAY BUSHNELL
ENTREPRENEUR

BORN: *February 5, 1943, Ogden*

Utahn Nolan Bushnell is best known for inventing the video game Pong in 1972. To market his new game, Bushnell founded the company Atari. Within a few years, more than one hundred thousand copies of Pong had been sold to bars and nightclubs. Other companies scrambled to copy Atari's success, and the video game revolution was born. Bushnell also launched the Chuck E. Cheese chain of restaurants.

TERRY TEMPEST WILLIAMS
ENVIRONMENTALIST

BORN: *1955, Corona, CA*

Author Terry Tempest Williams grew up within sight of the Great Salt Lake in Salt Lake City, Utah. She started her career as a children's author, winning a Children's Science Book Award from the New York Academy of Sciences for her book *The Secret Language of Snow*. She later began writing for an adult audience, tying personal and environmental issues together in her work. Williams' best-known book is *Refuge: An Unnatural History of Family and Place*, in which she examines the rise of the Great Salt Lake and her mother's death from cancer. Along with her environmental work, this book led to the recognition of Williams as a leading U.S. environmentalist.

DEBBI FIELDS
ENTREPRENEUR

BORN: *September 18, 1956, East Oakland, CA*

Entrepreneur Debbi Fields was born and raised in California. In 1977 she opened a small gourmet cookie store called Mrs. Fields Chocolate Chippery in a Palo Alto food court. The store was a success. Fields soon expanded her business to include other stores, and the Mrs. Fields Cookies retail chain was born. In 1982 Fields and her family moved to Park City, Utah. The Mrs. Fields Cookies corporate headquarters moved with them. During the years the company has been headquartered in Utah, Fields' empire has grown to include over seven hundred stores in twelve countries.

DONNY AND MARIE OSMOND
ENTERTAINERS

BORN: *December 9, 1957 (Donny) and October 13, 1959 (Marie), Ogden*

Donny and Marie Osmond were two of nine children in the Osmond family. Donny Osmond found success early as a singer with several of his brothers in a group called The Osmonds. Donny later teamed up with his sister Marie to produce new songs, with great success. They soon got an offer to host a TV variety show. *The Donny and Marie Show* was hugely popular for several years and is probably their best-remembered effort. After the show was canceled, Donny and Marie turned to a variety of movie, radio, TV, and charity jobs. Most recently, the duo hosted a TV talk show in the late 1990s and co-hosted two Miss America pageants.

Utah

History At-A-Glance

About 1350
Ancestors of present-day Native tribes arrive in the Utah area.

1776
Silvestre Vélez de Escalante and Francisco Atanasio Dominguez lead the first European expedition into present-day Utah.

1810
Mountain men become Utah's first non-Native residents.

1824
Mountain man Jim Bridger is the first non-Native to see the Great Salt Lake.

1830s
The U.S. government sends a series of expeditions to explore the Utah region.

1847
An advance party of Mormon settlers, led by Brigham Young, arrives at Salt Lake Valley.

1848
Mexico signs Treaty of Guadalupe Hidalgo, giving ownership of Utah region to United States.

1850
Mormons ask to join the Union as State of Deseret. Request denied. Utah Territory established instead.

1850s
Ute chief Wakara leads his people against the Mormons in the Walker War.

1857
President James Buchanan initiates the Utah War in an attempt to control Mormon settlers.

1861
The first telegraph line connecting the east and west coasts of the United States is completed in Salt Lake City.

1863
U.S. troops massacre 250 Shoshone at the Bear River Massacre.

1600   **1700**   **1800**

1492
Christopher Columbus comes to New World.

1607
Capt. John Smith and three ships land on Virginia coast and start first English settlement in New World — Jamestown.

1754–63
French and Indian War.

1773
Boston Tea Party.

1776
Declaration of Independence adopted July 4.

1777
Articles of Confederation adopted by Continental Congress.

1787
U.S. Constitution written.

1812–14
War of 1812.

United States

History At-A-Glance

1865–72
Ute chief Black Hawk leads bands of warriors against the Mormons in the Black Hawk War.

1869
The nation's first transcontinental railway line is completed with the driving of a gold spike at Promontory Point.

1882
The Edmunds Act imposes heavy fines on polygamists and takes away some of their rights.

1887
The Edmunds-Tucker Act strips the LDS Church of some of its property.

1890
LDS Church president Wilford Woodruff advises members to abandon the practice of polygamy.

1896
Utah is admitted to the Union as the forty-fifth state.

1906
Open-pit mining of copper begins at Bingham Canyon.

1929
The Great Depression leads to the temporary collapse of the Utah mining industry.

1931–32
A major drought drives thousands of Utah farmers to bankruptcy.

1941
U.S. entry into World War II gives a much-needed boost to Utah's economy.

1960–90
Tourism grows, becoming an increasingly important part of Utah's economy and bringing more outsiders to the state.

2002
Utah establishes itself as a world-class destination by hosting the Winter Olympic Games.

1800 — **1900** — **2000**

1848
Gold discovered in California draws eighty thousand prospectors in the 1849 Gold Rush.

1861–65
Civil War.

1869
Transcontinental railroad completed.

1917–18
U.S. involvement in World War I.

1929
Stock market crash ushers in Great Depression.

1941–45
U.S. involvement in World War II.

1950–53
U.S. fights in the Korean War.

1964–73
U.S. involvement in Vietnam War.

2000
George W. Bush wins the closest presidential election in history.

2001
A terrorist attack in which four hijacked airliners crash into New York City's World Trade Center, the Pentagon, and farmland in western Pennsylvania leaves thousands dead or injured.

▼ One of the main streets of Salt Lake City about 1900.

Festivals and Fun for All

Check web site for exact date and directions.

Cadillac Park City Art Festival,
Park City

Each year more than 100,000 visitors enjoy the work of hundreds of artisans at this nationally recognized outdoor art festival. Displays feature everything from fine art to cutting-edge and traditional craft.
www.kimball-art.org

Canyonlands Fat Tire Festival, **Moab**

Mountain bike enthusiasts gather at this international event, which includes trail rides, races, and related activities.
www.hometown.aol.com/eracerhd/fatfest.htm

Days of '47 Festivities,
Salt Lake City

Celebrate Utah's pioneer heritage, its settlers, and their difficult journey. The event features an art show, rodeos, and one of the largest and oldest parades in the United States.
www.daysof47.com

Easter Rendezvous, **Ogden**

A celebration of all things rugged that re-creates how Utah's first settlers lived. This gathering of modern-day mountain men features black-powder

shooting contests and other early nineteenth-century activities.
www.ogdencvb.org

Festival of the American West,
Wellsville

This event gives visitors a glimpse into the past with a re-created Native village, a mountain-man rendezvous, a military encampment, cowboy poetry readings, arts and crafts, and other traditional activities.
www.americanwestcenter.org

Living Traditions Festival,

Salt Lake City

More than forty area ethnic groups get together each year at this festival to celebrate Salt Lake City's diverse heritage. Visitors can experience Korean dancing, Peruvian crafts, Thai and Austrian food, and much more.
www.arts.utah.gov/folkarts/livingtraditions.html

Mormon Miracle Pageant,
Manti

A cast of more than five hundred actors reenacts the story of Jesus Christ, Joseph Smith, and the Mormon faith.
www.mormonmiracle.org

Timpanogos Storytelling Festival, Orem

With over twelve thousand people in attendance each year, this event is one of the largest storytelling festivals in the West.

www.timpfest.org

Utah Arts Festival, Salt Lake City

The multidiscipline Utah Arts Festival consistently ranks among the best arts events in the country. The festival features The Artists Marketplace, music, hands-on projects for kids and adults, and performing and literary arts.

www.uaf.org

Railroader's Festival, Brigham City

The Railroader's Festival commemorates the completion of the nation's first transcontinental railway. The Golden Spike Reenactment and spike-driving contests are the most popular parts of this annual celebration.

www.nps.gov/gosp/events/rrfest.html

Scandinavian Festival, Ephraim

Utahns celebrate their Scandinavian roots at this authentic and enthusiastic folk festival. Scandinavian foods, dances, and other activities bring Utah's ethnic heritage to life.

www.ephraimcity.com/recreation.html

Utah State Fair, Salt Lake City

Visitors get their fill of corn dogs, woolly sheep, and upside-down thrills at the annual Utah State Fair. Carnival rides, live entertainment, a horse show, a rodeo, livestock judging, and arts and crafts are all part of this event.

www.utah-state-fair.com

Ute Pow Wow, Fort Duchesne

Native tribes from all over the West attend this gathering, which features a rodeo, crafts, food, and traditional Ute activities.

www.dced.state.ut.us/indian/index.html

Sundance Film Festival, Park City

Considered one of the nation's premier film festivals, this event screens the very best of the year's independent films.

www.sundance.org

▶ The Sundance Institute was founded in 1981 by actor Robert Redford, who is shown in this photograph. The institute is dedicated to supporting independent filmmakers and showing their works at an annual Utah film festival.

Ute Stampede, Nephi

Cowboys and cowgirls compete to see who is the best of the best. Bull riding, bronc busting, calf roping, and other traditional rodeo contests test the skill of participants.

www.co.juab.ut.us/stampede/stampede.html

Books

Allen, John Logan. *Jedediah Smith and the Mountain Men of the American West*. New York: Chelsea House, 1991. Describes the explorations and exploits of famous explorers and trappers of the West.

Bushman, Claudia Lauper. *Mormons in America*. New York: Oxford University Press Children's Books, 1998. Focuses on the history, practices, and doctrines of the Church of Jesus Christ of Latter-day Saints.

Cushing, Raymond. *America's First Transcontinental Railway: A Pictorial History of the Pacific Railroad*. Pasadena, CA: Pentrex, 1994. Describes the construction of the first transcontinental railway from its eastern and western origins to its final joining at Promontory Point, Utah.

Flanagan, Alice K. *The Utes*. New York: Children's Press, 1998. Explains Ute traditions and cultures as well as the tribe's modern experiences.

Petersen, David. *Arches National Park*. New York: Children's Press, 1999. Describes the creation of the park, as well as its history, geology, and major features.

Rambeck, Richard. *Utah Jazz*. Mankato, MN: Creative Education, 1998. Details story of Utah's premier sports franchise.

Schleifer, Jay. *Bonneville!: Quest for the Land Speed Record*. Parsippany, NJ: Silver Burdett Press, 1995. All about Bonneville Salt Flats, the world's premier speed testing grounds.

Web Sites

▶ Official state web site
www.utah.gov

▶ Utah State Historical Society
www.history.utah.gov

▶ Utah travel information
www.utah.com

▶ Utah History Encyclopedia
www.media.utah.edu/UHE/UHEindex.html

Films and Documentaries

Emery, Shawn. *The Greatest Snow on Earth: Utah's Skiing Story*. Working Title Productions, 2002. Traces the history of skiing in Utah from the 1800s to the 2002 Winter Olympics.

Note: Page numbers in *italics* refer to maps, illustrations, or photographs.